Manifest YOUR Dreams

ART PROJECTS THAT INSPIRE

TONI BRODY

BALBOA.
PRESS

A DIVISION OF HAY HOUSE

Balboa Press books may be ordered through booksellers or by contacting:

Balboa Press
A Division of Hay House
1663 Liberty Drive
Bloomington, IN 47403
www.balboapress.com
1 (877) 407-4847

ISBN: 978-1-5043-5163-8 (sc)
ISBN: 978-1-5043-5164-5 (e)

Print information available on the last page.

Balboa Press rev. date: 04/08/2016

CONTENTS

To my husband,
Love you Baby

Welcome,

Thank you for choosing to bring these Art Projects into your life. They are meant to inspire you to focus on your goals and what you want to manifest into your reality by creating art projects you will display.

Each art project has a theme and questions to ask yourself regarding the theme. The answers to the theme questions will stimulate ideas you will use these ideas in your art projects.

When you finish creating, display the project in a prominent place where you can see it often. The images you have chosen of what you want to bring into your life are now part of the project. As you focus on the object of art your positive vibrations of what you want will rise.

A thought that is often repeated gains power and tends to come true.

Art experience is not necessary.

ABUNDANCE

Manifest Your Dreams – Art Projects that Inspire

Theme: Abundance

Art Projects:

52-Week Money Challenge

Abundance Bill

Make a Bank

Supplies for Abundance Projects:

Abundance Questions

List of things you want in abundance

Abundance Project Instructions

52-Week Challenge Chart/Google

Bank – Make using a box or purchase

Abundance Bill - Template No.01

Abundance

Abundance means a plentiful amount or fullness to overflowing.

Abundance Questions

1. I want a plentiful amount of?
2. I want an overflowing amount of?
3. I want a full supply of?

Abundance Project Instructions

1. Read the Abundance definition. Think about abundance and what it means to you. Answer the questions. Begin to make a list of things you would like to have in abundance. Look for images of the things you want keep them in a file. Use this list and images of what you want for ideas as you create your projects.

2. Create actual abundance by following the 52-week money challenge. Start by saving $1 the first week, the next week save $2, the third week save $3...and so on. There are charts available on Google. You will save $1,378.00 to buy something on the abundance list.

3. Create a bank using a cardboard box or purchase a bank for the 52-week challenge money. Decorate your bank with your favorite abundance words or draw images, glue magazine images, digital pictures, or other treasures you want onto or place inside of the bank.

4. Collect images of what you want in abundance. Make a copy of Abundance Bill Template No. 01, 1. Place a photo of yourself in the center area of the

Abundance Bill. Glue or tape the image into place. Add images of what you want in abundance on both sides of your image on the Abundance Bill. Cut the bill out. Place strips of clear tape carefully over the entire bill on both sides to protect it.

5. Display the Abundance Bill in a prominent place, focus on and enjoy the images of what you want. Save $1.00 a week for 52 weeks. At the end of the 52-week challenge there will be $1,378.00 in your bank. Review your list and pictures on your abundance bill to decide what to buy.

6. Say Thank You.

ATTRACTION

Manifest Your Dreams – Art Projects that Inspire

Theme: Attraction

Art Projects:

Attraction Box

License Plate for car or truck

Design Your Home

Supplies for Attraction Projects:

Attraction Project Instructions

What You Want to Attract List

Blank Box - Template No.02

Attract a New House - Template No. 03

Attract a Vehicle – License Plate - Template No. 04

Glue, pencils, markers, images

Attraction

Attraction – to draw to oneself with very specific and clear goals

Attraction Questions

1. I am visualizing myself in my new.
2. I have the ability to attract.
3. I have always wanted.

Attraction Project Instructions

1. Read the definition, answer the questions begin a list of what you want to attract and use the word because as you write why you want to attract "it" into your life.

2. Create a file of what you want. Find words and images that attract you, use them on your art projects to attract the things you want.

3. Copy Blank Box Template No. 02 on card stock or heavy paper. Decorate the Box with words and images of what you want to attract. Draw with pencil, and color with markers, stencils, glue on pictures, there are no limits so be creative. Cut out the box, fold, and sharp crease the edges, insert the tabs, and glue them into place. Let dry. Make an attraction box for everything you want to attraction and display them together. Focus on what you want.

4. Want to attract a new home or remodel an existing home? Copy House Template No. 03 Collect your ideas, paint samples for each room with pictures of furniture. The house template has 9 rooms. Name each room.

Decorate the 9-room home as yours will be when purchased or remodel completed. Decorate the outside of the home, walls, shutters, and curtains, create a yard. Display and feel yourself living there.

5. What would be on your personalized license plate of your new vehicle? Copy License Plate Template No. 04. License plates have seven spaces with numbers and letters alone or in combinations there are no limits. Be creative. Backgrounds are usually scenic or state related.

6. Ask, believe and you will receive. Explore the opportunities that come your way.

7. Say Thank You.

DESIRE

Manifest Your Dreams – Art Projects that Inspire

Theme: Desires

Art Project: Desires Tree

Supplies for Desires Project:

Desires Project instructions

Now, Later, and Long Term Desires List

Desires Tree - Template No. 05

Paints, color pencil, markers or crayons

Images of things you desire from magazines, words, and symbols.

Desire

Desire - To wish, long or crave for something

Desire Questions

1. What do I desire to do?
2. What do I long to own?
3. What do I crave?

Desires come and go all the time. Begin thinking about your desires. Organize your desires into 3 separate lists now, later and long-term desires. Keep your desires list up to date, cross off what you have received or no longer want and always add new desires as you think of them.

Desire Project Instructions

1. Read the Desires definition, answer the questions begin three separate lists each on its own full sheet of paper of what you want.

Organize your desires into 3 lists, 1. Desires you want NOW, immediately, that would make your life better. Desires you want LATER, what you will need in a few months or couple years. 3. Desires for the LONG TERM, things to make your life wonderful. Add hobbies, relationships, travel destinations, career, and anything you have ever desired. Do not limit yourself.

2. Copy the Desires Tree Template No. 05. Color your Desires Tree picture, sky first and in between fence posts, under the tree grass and flowers, fence, tree truck, branches and leaves, design the sign last. Title: My Desires, Desires Tree, or name of your choice.

3. After coloring the Desires Tree picture begin placing your desires on the Desires Tree. Desires may be portrayed as: Images, drawings, magazine pictures, symbols, stickers, bubble letters, hand written cursive. There are NO LIMITS.

4. Place your desires on the tree, fence, and sky in this order.

GROUND around the tree for the desires that are needed and wanted NOW, immediate.

TREE ROOTS, TRUNK AND LIMBS are for LATER desires as they rise.
FENCE is for those things you are not sure of yet that are ON THE FENCE.
TREE LEAVES - LONG TERM goals.
BETWEEN FENCE POSTS and SKY – Far Out desires

5. Obtaining your desires will bring you joy.

6. Say Thank You

FLOW

Manifest Your Dreams – Art Projects that Inspire
Theme: Flow
Art Project: Flow and Let Go

Supplies for Flow Project:
Flow Project Instructions
What you need to Allow to happen without your control
2 fine line permanent markers in different colors
Glossy ink jet photo paper

Flow – to move freely like a fluid, glide, drift, absorbed in an activity, hang loose

Flow Questions

1. Do I flow with life?
2. What am I trying to control that keeps me from flowing?
3. What things do I need to do to go with the flow of life?

There is no need for control, life is meant to be easy to flow. Many things will take care of themselves if we get out of our own way and the way of others. Learn to flow, take your mind off of your things and the things of others for just a moment and relax and breathe. This project has an easy flow to it that could be used to relax your breathing and as you make each line repeat to yourself, I am flowing or have a quiet mind breathing in calm and breathing out peace your life flowing with the lines.

Flow Project Instructions

1. Read the Flow definition, answer the questions. You can only control yourself or how you react to something that happens to you. Think about the people and life events you are trying to control.

2. This project uses contour lines. Contour lines are drawn as close together as possible without touching. Trace the outline of your hand including your fingers at least twice on a sheet of glossy ink jet photo paper using a black permanent marker. Trace you hands from different angles and overlap your fingers.

3. Choose 1 color marker for your hands, and another color marker for the background.

4. Begin drawing contour lines in the background start at the left edge of the paper. Draw a curved line, begin at the same left edge and draw another line following close but not touching the first line.

5. Continue drawing Contour *lines that follow as close to each other as possible without touching the same curve.* Relax, breathe and enjoy the process of flowing with the lines. Fill in the entire background.

6. Begin working contour lines inside the black outline of your hands. Start at the wrist; decide on the angle of the first contour line. Continue adding contour lines until all the hands and fingers are all filled in.

7. Flow and enjoy your life experiences and allow others to enjoy theirs.

8. Say Thank You.

GRATITUDE

Manifest Your Dreams – Art Projects that Inspire

Theme: Gratitude

Art Projects: Gratitude Journal and Personalized Pen

Supplies for Gratitude Journal:

Spiral bound composition notebooks (any size)

Paper for marbling, any type

Can of shave cream, foam not gel

Liquid acrylic paints in drip bottles

Containers for shave cream the size of the composition notebook

Scrapers, or side of sturdy cardboard

Glues, markers, scissors, embellishments of your choosing

Supplies for Personalized Pen

Ink pen - Florist tape – embellishments, silk flowers

Gratitude

Gratitude – is gratefulness, appreciation and thankfulness

Gratitude Questions

1. What do I already have that I give thanks for?
2. I am very appreciative that I am?
3. Thank You everyday for my?

Think about gratitude and the list of people, places and things that you are grateful for everyday. Review your past and list people, places and things that were instrumental in you being you today.

Gratitude Project Instructions

Read the Gratitude definition answer the questions and start thinking about the people, places and things that have helped to make you. Organize your information starting from Birth, were you born, teachers, mentors, schools you attended, colleges, jobs, careers, family, education, and street experience. The Accumulation of experiences on the list is what makes you who you are today. The list is endlessly full of people you owe gratitude.

1. The goal of this project is to produce marbled papers to decorate and use, as special inserts into the personal journal and to decorate a ballpoint pen to write the things you are grateful for in the journal and on the marbled papers. Cut to fit and glue the marbled papers onto the front and back of the composition notebook short of the spiral binding, Cut the rest of the marbled papers into strips and shapes to use for bookmarks, reminders, and notes, inserts, stickers, backgrounds for your journal entries.

2. Save discarded newspaper, a table covering you can throw away, aluminum or plastic containers the size of your composition notebook, cans of shave cream, scrapers, cardboard edges to scrape shave cream from paper, garbage bag for all the mess.

3. Paper Marbling - This is *messy*, but is great fun and very stress relieving.

4. Spray the shave cream about ¼ of an inch thick (any brand, foam not gel) into a container large enough for your paper to flatten on top of the shave cream.

5. Drip acrylic paint on top of the shave cream. Use forks, toothpicks, to swirl in a design

6. Place the paper on top of shave cream; lightly rub the papers back to make sure the paper has contact with the shave cream.

7. Remove the paper by pulling the paper up gently using one of the corners.

8. Place the marbled paper in the center of open layers of disposable newspaper.

9. Use a scraper (stiff cardboard) to scrape the shave cream and paint off of the paper. Clean the scraper on the newspaper, putting the shave cream in the folds of the newspaper. Repeat the process with different colors of acrylic paint on clean shave cream. Continue to marble paper until you have marbled enough paper to use to decorate your journal.

***CLEAN-UP
SCRAPE SHAVE CREAM INTO FOLDS OF NEWSPAPER. DO NOT - DO NOT PUT THE SHAVE CREAM DOWN THE DRAIN

10. Glue the marbled papers on to the composition notebooks front and back inside and outside covers, personalize journal and marbled papers to use as inserts, note pads, stickers, dividers, and bookmarks for your Gratitude Journal. Use markers, pencils, add embellishments.

Personalized Pen

Supplies needed:

Ballpoint pen – florist tape – silk flower embellishments

1. Read the directions on the florist tape.

2. Wrap the pen starting at the tip used for writing to almost the end with tape. Wrap the tape tightly around the pen.

3. Leave the very top of the pen without tape to add decorations that will be wrapped inside of the tape

4. Wrap silk flower stems in side of the florist tape at the top of the pen. Be creative.

5. Copy or place the list of people, places, and things you are grateful for into your journal. Add why you are grateful for these things. Gratitude = a sense of being thankful for...

6. Say Thank You

LOVE

Manifest Your Dreams – Art Projects that Inspire
Theme: Love
Arts Project: ALL the Letters in Your Name

Supplies for Love Project:
Love Project Instructions
List of reasons to love and appreciate yourself
Blank paper
Pencils, markers

Love – fondness, tenderness, affection

Love

1. Who Do I love most in the world??
2. Do I think of myself as I do him/her?
3. Do I think of myself with tenderness or affection?

Love Project Instructions

1. This project uses all of the letters in your name. You can use sir names; nicknames, pet names, and any *nice* names you are called or you call yourself. The object is to get you thinking about you and appreciating you by creating an abstract design with your name. If using more than one name complete each name.

2. Name Design Number 1. Start any place on a blank sheet of paper. Draw the first letter of the name you are going to use with an outline shape, upper and lower case, any writing style you choose. Turn the paper and draw the second letter of the same name touching the first letter, the letters should touch each other to close off the spaces. Make the letter in different sizes and slant some of the letters. Keep turning the paper and adding more names and letters. Fill in entire page with letters of positive names you are called.

3. Name Design Number 2. Make another name design using the same name used on the 1st name design or other positive names you are called..

4. You now have 2 name designs to color.

5. The first name design color the BACKGROUND ONLY

6. The second name design color the LETTERS ONLY.

7. As you color your name design you will create two beautiful images that represent you. Display the images, admire the beauty of the name design as you love and appreciate yourself

8. Say Thank You

NATURE

Manifest Your Dreams – Art Projects that Inspire

Theme - Nature

Art Project: Nature Circle

Supplies for Nature Project:

Nature Project Instructions

What You Enjoy in Nature List

Nature Circle Information

Circle Template No. 06

Nature

Nature – the world of living things and the outdoors, earth, globe, cosmos, universe

Nature Questions

1. I enjoy nature the most when?
2. What effect does the outdoors have on me?
3. What is my connection to other living things?

Nature Project Instructions

1. Think about what YOU appreciate in nature and what nature does for you. Natural High, Sense of Connection, Exercise, Stress Reduction, Respect for Nature, Animal Awareness, Quiet, Breathing, Spiritual Benefits, Healing. Organize your information into thoughts of the months of the year, seasons - summer, fall, winter, spring, zodiac signs and symbols and their meanings your favorite nature pictures, signs, and symbols.

2. Copy the Circle Template No. 06. Follow the directions to complete the nature circle.

3. *Center circle* - The sun - draw the sun, use words, paint, or glue on a picture of the sun.

4. *Four spaces* surrounding the sun - four seasons: summer, fall, winter, spring. Add pictures of the seasons and how the seasons make you feel.

5. *12 areas* around the seasons are for the months of the year - zodiac signs, birthstones, symbols, names and birthdays, anything about the zodiac, elements for each month. Zodiac signs and dates - Aries -March 21-April 19, Taurus – April 20- May 20, Gemini – May 21- June 20, Cancer – June 21- July 22, Leo – July 23 – August 22, Virgo – August 23 – September 22, Libra – September 23 – October 22, Scorpio – October 23 – November 21, Sagittarius – November 22 – December 21, Capricorn – December 22 – January 19, Aquarius – January 20 – February 18, Pisces – February 19 – March 20

6. Outside border is free space to decorate or add more nature information.

7. Say Thank You.

NOW

Manifest Your Dreams – Art Projects that Inspire

Theme: Now

Arts Project: Coat of Arms

Supplies for Now

Now Project Instructions

What is going on in My Life Now list

Coat of Arms Template No. 07

Now

Now – At the present time, current, living in the moment

Now Questions

1. The best thing happening right this second is?
2. What good things are happening in my daily life?
3. My now is wonderful because?

Now Project Instructions

1. Living in the moment is called mindfulness a state of active, open, intentional attention on the present. Take your time and start small answering the coat of arms questions.

2. Copy the Coat of Arms Template No. 07. Place the information onto the coat of arms starting from the top left space and ending with the scroll at the bottom use images, symbols, and words.

   a. Things you do for fun.
   b. Things you plan to explore.
   c. Complete the following I AM... with positive words
   d. Words to describe your inner self.
   e. Positive words you would like to hear said about you.
   f. Career /Job/Work/Hobby.
   g. Free space be creative.
   h. Heritage examples.
   i. Environment examples.

j. Accomplishments you are proud of.

k. Your personal mascot or symbol.

3. Motto or words you live by on the bottom scroll.

4. Display the Coat of Arms, be mindful of the wonderful things happening to you now.

5. Say Thank You

SECRETS

Manifest Your Dreams - Art Projects that Inspire

Theme: Secrets

Arts Project: Marker Scribble

Supplies for Secrets Project:

Secrets Project Instructions

Secrets definition

Scribble Template No. 08

Thin markers, no. 2 pencil, and large eraser

Secrets

Secret – keeping knowledge to ones self, concealed from others

Keeping secrets or living a secret life provokes inner conflict that can lead to anxiety, chronic worry and unhealthy conditions.

Secret Questions

1. What are my secrets?
2. Why am I keeping this in myself?
3. I release myself from…

Secrets Project Instructions

1. Think about secrets; things that happened in your life that cause you any type of guilt, or anxiety. These events could be known by others or known only to you, perceived and negative things you whisper in your mind about yourself.

2. Copy the Scribble Template No. 08 or make your own scribble on paper use permanent marker. Write all of your secrets in the many spaces on the scribble template with a no. 2 pencil. Use code words, symbols, write backwards, any crazy way you can for privacy.

3. Use colorful permanent markers to create scribble designs all OVER AND ON TOP OF the secrets in each of the spaces.

4. Mindfully cover over the secrets in each space with different colors lines, patterns, create your own designs. The secrets will disappear under the marker and become part of a beautiful vibrant design.

5. Take your time. When your marker designing is complete use a large pencil eraser to ERASE all of the secrets.

6. One space at a time, erase the secrets releasing yourself as they disappear from your life.

7. Say Thank You

SELF LOVE

Manifest Your Dreams – Art Projects that Inspire

Theme: Self Love

Arts Projects:

Handwriting Cube

Self Love Cube

Supplies for Self Love Cubes

Self love project information

Positive Words list

2 Blank Box Templates No. 02 – copied on card stock

Markers, scissors, glue or clear tape

Self Love

Self love - The desire to promote ones own interest or well being

Handwriting – The writing done with the hand typical of a particular person

Self Love Questions

1. Who do I love?
2. Do I love myself as much as I love?
3. Do I feel selfish when I love myself?

Self-Love Project Instructions

Who do you love the most in your life? You should love yourself as much as you love this person. Self-love is not a form of selfishness. Loving the self communicates gratitude to whatever force gives us life. You are not able to truly love another until you love yourself.

Begin a list of positive words. Appealing, Beautiful, Colorful, Exciting, fashionable, Fun, Free, Gentle, Interesting, Clear, Charming, Enough, Safe, Love, Smart, Wonderful, Shy, Super, Joy, Peace, Open, Plenty, Curious, Fortunate, Happy, Youthful, Vibrant, Success, Wealthy, Vital, Thankful, Strong, Classy, Excited.

Enjoy your personal style of handwriting as you create the positive word list.

1. Make another positive list of words about yourself. Use a dictionary and thesaurus. Be mindful of your handwriting as you create the list. Practice your letters upper and lower case. Write your signature noticing how you

write each letter. On a separate sheet of paper write yourself a positive word letter sending love to you. Grateful for all the wonderful things you have done in your life so far.

2. Copy Box Template No. 02. Write your name on the box first name in one direction. Last name in the other direction; the names will cross over each other. Design around your name with markers or color pencils following the lines of your handwriting, enjoy the flow of the color around the letters your name.

3. Copy Box Template No. 02. This box is for Positive Words to say about you. Review the list of positive words in the self-love information and review the positive word list you have completed. Write IAM anywhere on the box place positive words about you on the remainder of the spaces on the box in all directions and in every space. Say each positive word about yourself as you write the word. Design around the words with colored pencils and markers.

4. Display the boxes flat or cut the box out, fold along lines, tape or glue into a cube shape.

5. Say Thank You to you

STRESS RELEASE

Manifest Your Dreams – Art Projects that Inspire

Theme: Stress Release

Corresponding Art Project: Stress Release Dart Circle

Supplies for Stress Release Project:

Stress Release Project Instructions

List of your stress releasers

Stress Template No. 09

Stress Release

Stress – strain, tension, anxiety, burden, pressure,

1. What causes you frustration and negative emotional feelings?
2. Where do you constantly run into aggravation?
3. Which areas of your life do you feel the most hurt or disappointed?

Release – let loose, untie, dismissal

1. What helps me to release stress?
2. I am relaxed when I am?
3. I feel less burdened when?

Create a list of activities, environments, music, books, magazines, parks, and any type of stress release that will work for you.

Stress Relievers

Always have a plan B, Write things down, Know you did the right thing, Become a listener, Get a hug, Avoid negative people, Believe in you, Be aware of decisions, Dance, Exercise, Just do it, Say, I don't know, Ask for help, Take time for you, Sleep, Laugh a lot, Make Art, Say, no more often, Set priorities, Don't procrastinate, Simplify, Unclutter your life, Stop planning, Comedy, Sit by a fire, Listen to music, Be mindful, Allow, Get a Massage, Read, Breathe, Say Yes more, Smile, Flirt, Say Thank You, Calm mind, Let go, Deep breathing, Write it down, Make copies, Clean, Go natural, Schedule, Unclutter, Short term goals, Look at art. Releasing stress will make you healthier.

Stress Release Project Instructions

1. You are going to create a dart circle of stress releasers. When you are stressed look at the circle choose the stress releasers that catches your eye first. Just looking at the dart circle reading the stress releaser will release your stress and cause you to breathe. Create a list of what relaxes you, settles you down allows you to breathe and release your stress

2. Print out the Stress Template No. 09. Write the word Breathe in the center circle because when you are stressed are you not breathing correctly.

3. The dart circle has 36 spaces divided into 12 areas with three different sizes. Begin with the 12 large areas write words for the stress releasers that work the fastest. Make the letters bold, vibrant and in your favorite colors. These will always catch your eye.

4. The smaller areas above and below the main releaser spaces are for secondary stress releasers. These smaller areas for stress release will catch your eye when you have more time to focus on and read your dart circle. Color the lettering and or spaces around the lettering in ways that will get your attention.

5. Display the dart circle in a place you usually feel stressed. When you feel stress beginning to build, look at your dart circle chose a release. Implement the stress releaser immediately. Optional – Purchase darts cut out the dartboard, spin, you know the rest.

6. Breathe and say Thank You.

WEALTH

Manifest Your Dreams - Art Projects that Inspire

Theme: Wealth

Art Project: Personal, Material and Spiritual Wealth Wheel

Supplies for Wealth Project:

Wealth Template No. 10

Pencil and eraser

Press and stick letters

Color markers

Black Marker for outlining letters

Wealth

Personal – exclusive, private, own, individual

Spiritual – supernatural, metaphysical, otherworldly, innermost, intangible

Material – matter, substance, stuff, facts, figures, data

Wealth Information

Three types of Wealth

Personal Wealth - what means the most to you.

Material Wealth - possessions, riches.

Spiritual Wealth - inside that no one can take away.

Wealth Questions

1. What are my views on wealth?
2. How often do I think about wealth?
3. In what ways am I already wealthy?

Wealth Project Instructions

1. Read the Wealth information. Answer the questions begin three separate lists.

1. Spiritual wealth 2. Personal Wealth 3. Material wealth. Use the wealth definition information explaining the different types of wealth to help you determine which is personal, material or spiritual wealth to you.

2. Copy the Wealth Wheel Template No. 10. Write the word wealth in the center circle. Choose a separate color for each type of wealth.

3. The wealth wheel is split into three rings the ring closest to the center circle is the smallest ring and should be filled with words of the wealth least important to you. The largest ring is in the middle fill it with words for your most important wealth. Finally the outer ring is for the wealth that is in your middle. Fill each ring with personal wealth, spiritual wealth, and material wealth words. Some material wealth can be spiritual and/ or personal. Make your word lists and take your time deciding. Display the Wealth Wheel enjoying the abundance you already have.

4. Say Thank You.

Project Templates– Templates are re-useable, please make copies.

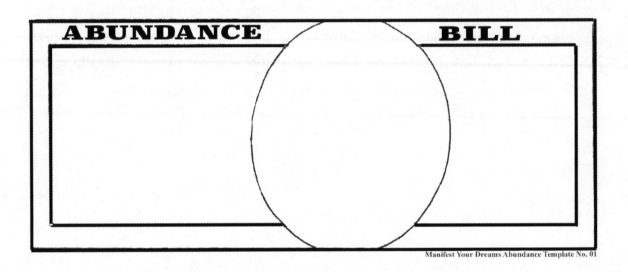

Manifest Your Dreams Abundance Template No. 01

Manifest Your Dreams - Abundance Bill

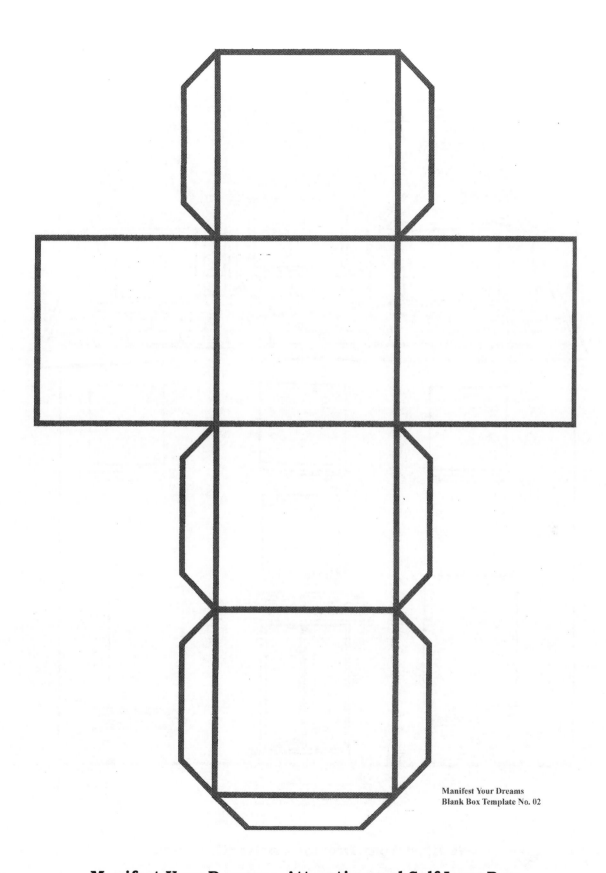

Manifest Your Dreams
Blank Box Template No. 02

Manifest Your Dreams - Attraction and Self Love Box

Manifest Your Dreams
House Template No. 03

Manifest Your Dreams - Attraction House

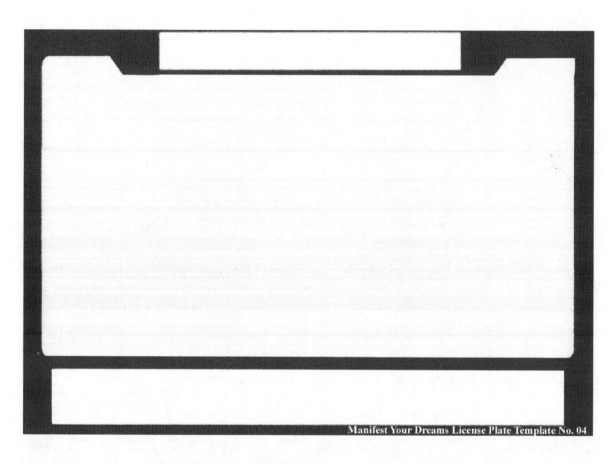

Manifest Your Dreams License Plate Template No. 04

Manifest Your Dreams - License Plate

Manifest Your Dreams
Desires Tree Template No. 05

Manifest Your Dreams - Desire Tree

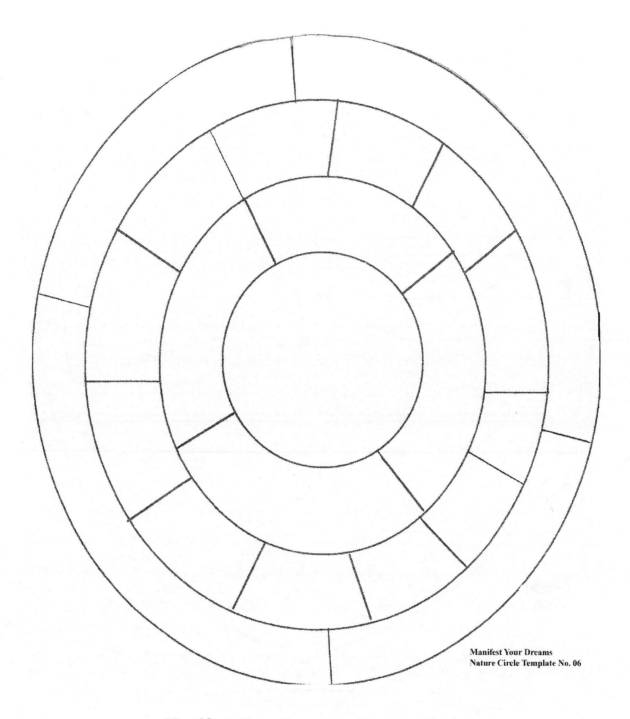

Manifest Your Dreams
Nature Circle Template No. 06

Manifest Your Dreams - Nature Circle

43

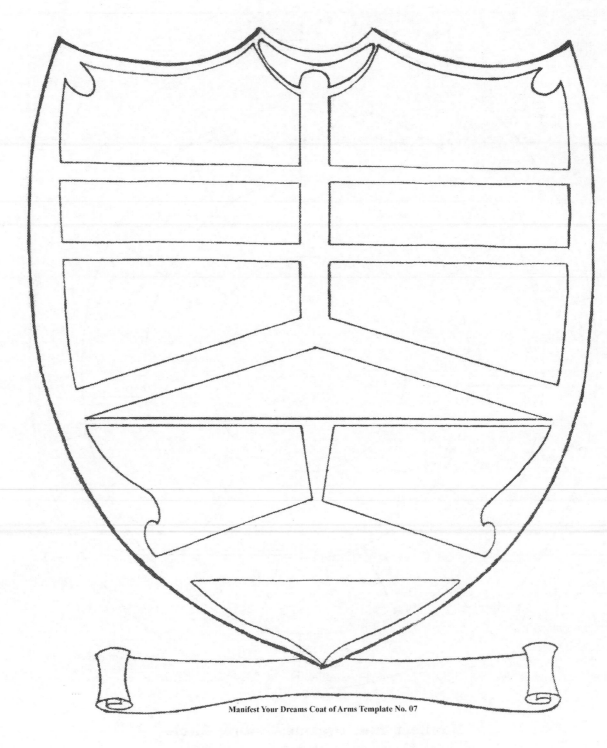

Manifest Your Dreams Coat of Arms Template No. 07

Manifest Your Dreams - Coat of Arms

44

Manifest Your Dreams
Secrets Template No. 08

Manifest Your Dreams - Secrets Scribble

45

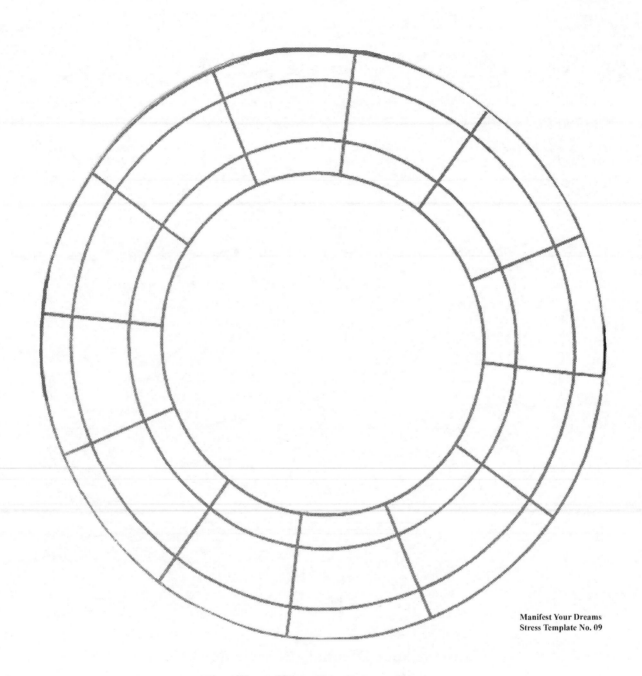

Manifest Your Dreams
Stress Template No. 09

Manifest Your Dreams – Stress

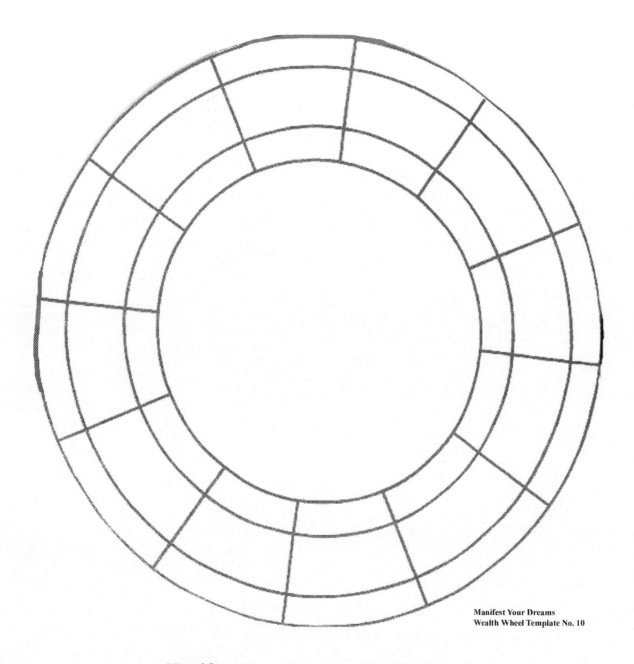

Manifest Your Dreams – Wealth Wheel